D1094707

JOSEPH'S SON

SHEILA MOON

JOSEPH'S SON

THE GOLDEN QUILL PRESS
Publishers
Francestown   New Hampshire

Standard Book Number 8233-0172-9

Second printing May 1973

Printed in the United States of America

For

Elizabeth

without whose love, wisdom and faith
this book would not exist. In
truth, it is hers.

Contents

JOSEPH'S SON

PROLOG

(1)

Such macrocosmic motes
as drift and spin in black space
beyond our remaining hills
are of less moment than how
turning enters a man,
how a slow year comes alone
to a man, to Man,
warming himself under Orion.
Universes may be bright or dead,
may have lived and ended
in incandescence, in cold snow,
be going mute through time
flowing interminably into itself;
and man be time's absurd King,
coloring his Kingdom with himself,
trying to outwit brevity with fire.
Whether he goes or does not go
beyond orbits of day-night-day
to some similar earth, if he is lost
he will be lost, here or there.
And if he turns, can learn
to wrestle his desire another way,
can face it around to see its eyes,
here or there, why then he will turn.
Those other places — hanging stars
or canyons of the sea — are not so wise

nor as far as what he yearns for
when he considers his season.

(2)

Of course he's time's idiot as well.
Watch him perform his campaigns
and reprisals on an earth he longs
to inherit, with flames to prove it
belongs to him. To him, no more
durable than a May fly, his death
so near his birth he scarcely
knows he's been a fact!
How can he act to turn, then,
wringing his hands as the years
slow down? He dreads so much.
Even his love is wide-eared, staring,
wild in flight from ancient foes
like pity and a chill sky.
Filled with guilt for deeds,
for non-deeds, and for being done
or undone. he runs up the clock
to an unplanned, striking, stinking end.
So how can he turn, how not
be bent by doubt when dying's
his dearest twin from the womb?
Much that's lovely will outlast
his vulnerable flesh: those stones;
that mountain multigreen
at its blue edge; Chartres, her sisters,

and their vehement grace; man's song
hewn from his loneliness; every
product of his incredible hands;
what he has found and cherished,
tried to save, mourned, made
strong again. They watch him die.

(3)
There are a few who, during spans
of historied man's harvest,
have risked a fuller fruit, have
plunged to blind ground
and left behind the rasping years.
True was their descent, asked
by itself only, plumb line straight,
smashing at midnight
in a bright bloody river of seed.
Such men have turned, have lent
their flesh to needs of earth,
to life wanting birth and tomorrow.
They are wanderers. They bear questions
fresh with asking and desire
toward always a farther garden.
They come from nowhere, their home
is sorrow, their eyes hear gold
and their ears see dreams. They
yearn for points of fire unborn,
above each abyss they brood light
and follow smallest gleam on feet

burning with love. What is this
they do? What breach in our walls
comes with their coming, to let
into our prison the smell of sun
and grass? Their existence tells
itself to ours through the crack.
One such was Jesus the Jew, bearing
his hours on his back, — pedlar
of choices and fisher for God.
Let him pass.

I CAME TO JOHN

Through fierce-starred midnights
and searing noondays I walked Judea,
filled with memories of Nazareth's wood,
its smell, its live grain, its warmth under my hands;
filled with words of prophets
crying my people's kingdom for generations.
            Doubts circled me in darkness
— staring, waiting, unsleeping beasts —
then pursued me silent-footed under the sun
until I wanted to shout them away!
For who can endure God's coming?
Who can stand when he appears?
But through dust, loneliness, stars, heat,
I heard always
        Return to me, and I will return to you.
How should I return, I asked, sand in my mouth.
Dry hours gave no answer.
I stumbled the Judean plain to Jordan's reedy edge.
There—seeing the Baptist's sparse and ragged presence,
face furrowed with fasting, hearing him
rasp his apocalypse into a burning sky
— there I learned.
God's needs were into my flesh like thorns
(never after to leave me),
and Adam, Cain, Jacob, Noah, Job
— each was a necessity of God to be more full
than law or desire or wrath.

                                    I saw
God's need and mine to find each other
hurled in John's angry cry,
'Bear fruit that befits repentance!'
I plunged until yellow waters shut out the world.
Water-sound roared about me
and waves of my life rushed past
blown by great winds. I was alone
in creation's abyss where Spirit moved
and thundered for light,
Let there be light!
                              There was light . . .
Astarte's gentle bird, earth-finder,
compass of olive branch, Noah's dove —
she came to my wet hands — a reply
to previous thunder of penitential floods.
Her heart's pulse was love,
and I was parented and born in her voice,
that very day, to a kingdom
different than any had supposed.

WILDERNESS

How I had come here to this harshness of stone,
unweathered in raw light,
and sand blown into riffles,
and a few angular underfed bushes,
did not concern me.
I'd seen my sandal tracks;
they had led me to Moses
— Moses banned from Lebanon
but shouting his visions and commands to Israel,
Moses seeing the Lord his God as great and terrible,
a fire merciless as this present desert.
I thought of Moses dying in Moab,
and of myself familiar in Nazareth,
both of us fate-crossed at the same ugly river.
A lizard fled from sunless stone to wherever lizards go,
while I pulled my worn robe
closer over my shoulders. It would be cold again,
and hunger be more naked, I guessed,
as I shifted against the rock to ease my back.
        Love, and being beloved,
clung to the air everywhere around me —
even after all this time —
and my turtledove repeated herself shyly in darkness.
These things were my own, had happened to me
        forever.
Where I must take them or be taken by them
— well, I would understand or be destroyed!

Sunlight had been crueler today.
My eyes gritted and ached from it;
night should be comfort but was not.
Tonight stars burst and burned holes in space.
And now my body shook; earth tossed me.
I stumbled onto a black stage where
Moses and the Baptist argued God and wrath,
where I was flayed by both.
                    I tried to run
but another seized me, saying,
"Beloved and newly born, Israel once had manna
from God! Why not again! Why not from you?"
Manna there had been, and fire by night
and water from rocks! Why not, I thought,
for all my people and me?
                    Then Moses' words came clear:
He humbled you and let you hunger.
Know in your heart that as a father disciplines his son,
so does the Lord your God to you.
                    I twisted away,
staring into deeper dark. My hands,
clutched to each other, prisoned my face.
The other grasped me, saying,
                    "Beloved and newly born,
government can be upon your shoulders and Israel
          triumph!"
The kingdoms and cities glowed beneath me,
power lifted my head, my hand
reached for captives' hands outstretched —

But Moses' words cried out:
You shall fear the Lord your God!
You shall serve Him and swear by His name!
      Shame swept me with abrasive wind;
memory of love pulled me to coarse sand
under my knees; dove's wisdom returned me
to Jordan's purgation.
I must not forget that dialog
given in water-jeweled light!
Nor escape that son! I closed my eyes for peace.
But stars flamed through my flesh,
and inside my eyelids I could see Jerusalem
proud and moonlit, her templed heights
cleaving Roman earth, carrying Abraham's rock
as a testament; and I saw myself upcast
to the temple's zenith where that other
clutched at me, whispering,
                 "Beloved
and newly born, first inheritor, dare to be
Adonai's law. Praise him and prove him
for his passion declared."
Across black skies I saw the Day Star flare,
myself vertiginous, falling, aware of hordes
fleeing reeling Jerusalem, of men
blown by cruel winds to bones and dust.

Abrupt silence rejoined me to known night
and wilderness.
         Then my own cracked voice was saying,

"So teach us to number our days . . ."
And I was tasting the ancient words,
"My refuge and my fortress . . ."
and I heard
"Because he cleaves to me in love, I will deliver
        him . . ."

And I slept a circle of time,
dreaming of messengers, bleached bones and prophets,
dreaming of doves and birth. I wakened.
I moved with sure fierce love towards Galilee.

A HANDFUL OF FISHERMEN

Galilean hills are modest.
They uphold ancient existences of olive trees
like a blue mist, have square spindly sheep;
they fold into fissures and wrinkles;
they flare out for straw-colored towns,
and villages odorous and rackety
with begetting, food, quarreling, death.
Nazareth is such. When I returned to her,
wilderness still feathered my ears
and my feet were yet bright
with freedom between God and me.
Power of having chosen was a bursting joy
toward everyone as I jostled my ascent home.
An empty shop's wood greeted me —
sweet smell, firm skin under my fingers,
plough handle and upright post half-done,
ready for smoothing, hammer and nails
laid by in a tumble of shavings.
So had our Sabbath ever been, quiet, warm,
disheveled. And always Nazareth's Sabbath
sounded loud! Lamentations,
camel-songs spiraling dusty air,
cries of children — all these were usual
as sunset and shofar.
                        But when I came again
unsayable fullness hurt my throat,
my hands ached from holding;

unlike what I had been as Joseph's shy son,
I walked large with prophets to synagogue.
There Isaiah's words
leaped into my voice, saying,
The Spirit of the Lord God is upon me . . .
                    While ancient words unrolled,
inward I saw Jordan, river and desert,
and inward heard my dove, and inward knew
why Nazareth and I, despite our desires,
could never heal each other.
I left, seeing my father throw his heart
after me — but he was a fine carpenter
and needed here. He had a family to hold to.
As I descended my village eastward
my sandals slapped stones and darkening echoes
stammered against shut doors.

                    Sun rushes
into the lake of Gennesaret on fair mornings
as if it had never happened before!
It glistens on surfaces.
Each wave has a piece of sun on its tip,
and fisher's boats with gay sails
ride in puddles of silver. Shepherds
and sheep on green slopes are flushed
in sunrise, while rushes stand
leaning into day with slivers of brightness
on their fuzzed edges. Since my thin days
of youth — of driving wood-laden asses

homeward in smoky autumn afternoons,
of gathering a fistful of threshed wheat
from a harvest, of pulling myself
up into some fig-tree's shade to gorge
on purple sweets — then and since
I had been drawn always to this sea.
Nazareth crowded me. Now I needed space
and man's heartbeats gathered together.
Cool Capernaum had both.
I slept near her walls at water's edge.
I went in and out of her gates
in throngs of strangers and beasts.
I sat under date-palms and ate begged bread
and olives, pondering what grew in me
since the Baptist. On Sabbaths I went
to Capernaum's synagogue, heavy, dark,
smelling of sacrifice, incense, the sea.
My eyes sought other's eyes and faces
and found them shouting at me
with pain I could scarcely hold,
sharp as nails driven into my flesh.
Madmen, because I loved them
and their countenanced terror,
because I knew their desolation as my own,
returned to peace, calling me a Holy One of God.
And many came crying,
bringing fear in their fevered hands,
distrust heavy on their backs.
Because I saw them and let them in

(for who could not be in this kingdom?)
they marveled, they stood straight,
they sang loud and followed me
as if I were their life.
I recalled that other
who had tried me in the wilderness and lost.
I took myself far beyond men's reach
and gathered my truth into Isaiah's vision:
Enlarge the site
of your tent, and stretch without limit
the curtains of your home.

Galilee's sea was gray-green and lilac
seen from hills above Tiberias,
with fat clouds, dark-keeled, riding
heavily across, wind pushing white water against
rocked margins.
I leaned into it downslope,
wanting to run into its freshness and sea-smell
to defer those acts already chosen.
But I came quiet
to a blown shore where round bottoms of boats
upturned into storm's approach,
and a handful of fishermen amid their nets
were splendid in work and sunburnt laughter.
We shared bread, olives, wine,
and boat's shelter in a brief wild rain.
Some heard my passion, and came along into mist
and twilight to help my world's birth.

CONVERSATIONS ON THE SON OF MAN

Ezekiel:
    I found him in a God-fisted storm
with a rush of eagles, bellowing bulls,
lion's roar, and the shout of a man
above all thunder and fire!
The Lord Yahweh hurled me to my feet
in a dazzle of sapphire and bronze loins,
of wings and wheels blowing worlds to nothing!

Daniel:
    I found him in Babylon
in dark dreams crueler than my lions —
horned beasts and kings devoured,
destroying, stirring sea's cauldron
to fierce froth engulfing Belshazzar's glories.
I was afraid and troubled
before judgments of immensity.

Jesus:
    I found him in a turbid river
and a dove's song, in repentance
and a rock-raw wilderness
where animals and others watched.
With Jerusalem before me,
I knew what he was not. I was learning him.

Ezekiel:
     You cannot! He is a mouth
for the Lord God already learned!
A watchman over rebel Israel!

Jesus:
     Closer to Jeremiah's covenant.
Written upon men's hearts
blood-red as each spring's poppies.
And more. Somewhere love intrudes.

Daniel:
     Only the Lord's. Not his.
Before Ancient of Days he stands,
small in his dominion
and suppliant under a terrible burning throne
whose judge will atomize nations.
Yet he is greatly beloved by the Lord,
Gabriel says, telling a world's death.

Jesus:
     Beloved is a state of ends
and beginnings, not death.
Only when beginning's beginning
to rot from the hard core
may fruit at last prove itself.
He is always dear — sought and secured each day
like a kernel of sun lifted
from dark ground.

Ezekiel:
   He is huge!
His shadow uses me
and is used by Israel's God!
I am encompassed,
I become the son of man serving words of the Lord
to an unrighteous people! I carry
an exile's baggage, speaking against
prophets, making riddles and lamentations,
preaching a wrathful sword
and writing down God's anguish!

Daniel:
   Coming late to my dreams,
he is, as he is mine, burdened
by things to come. Since Gabriel gave me
the son of man, I am not as I was
under kings. Less sleep. Less peace.
Strengthened, though, with new wisdom.

Jesus:
   God's long loneliness,
seeking since Adam to father love
equal to creation, becomes a son of Man
wherever man will take him as a work
to do. Few will. Few care to shoulder God,
to lift burdens of forgiveness,
or choice, or unsheltered journeys
to painful dawns. Few dare to swallow

Jonah's black waters. When you do —
O Ezekiel, then truly the son of Man
is a ripe storm! And still as a seed,
Daniel, small as a mustard grain.
With myself, yourself, with man's self
the fertile lightning-ploughed sprouting ground
for God's becoming.

WHAT SETS A MAN FREE?

The dream flashed storm,
crashed against me like a bronze bell,
and I leapt awake to see familiar bundles
of sleeping comrades, with cypress
and fig-tree brushing cold still stars.
What rested out there in darkness,
head on paws, until I called it?
What had cried? Of all who met
and compassed us daily with needs
loud and rough as crows, who heard?
    Samuel, innocent Samuel,
had heard and had answered. Samuel
knew in part. But had he seen, ever,
the many-headed beasts riding fire,
the weighty thrones, the plains
of jewels and skeletons? Ezekiel
had seen. And heard, "Son of man, stand
upon your feet and I will speak with you!"
Ezekiel risked. Learned to say riddles.
He also would have known. In part.
But I called my dream
(beast, thrones, voice) in with day,
and we went into Capernaum's alleys.
Echoes and smells of asses, men, dream,
sheep, surrounded us. We became a shore.
Waves of people pounded us,
and broke, and hissed away, over and over.

I was an island in a flood tide,
eyes and mouths rising to cover me.
I was swept along and into a house,
crowded, packed down
and spilling out with contentious despair.
A roof-hole opened.
Down a slant of dusty sunlight,
slow, like a net returning unwanted fish,
a roped pallet drifted and settled before me.
Those eyes in that fearful face
were damped fires needing wind to flame them,
so I blew that necessary wind,
somewhat from prophets, somewhat from my dream.
"Stand," I said to the man.
"Stand and go free." The face melted
to another design and thin arms pushed
to lift, until at last on spindle legs
wobbly as a foal's, a bent smile
across his fear, his friends led him away.

      For those who maligned all choice
and inward acts, who held
law above growth and love
as lesser than mastery, there were no possibles,
I thought, as I lay bathed in night
and sea-smells. As I fell asleep
I imagined a colt's whinny,
and hoofbeats awkward on a spring field.

JAMES IS AFRAID

Far-sighted fishermen wander easily,
having lived always under dominion
of what cannot be held, never sure
whether silver-sided fish will flash
under a boat's keel at daybreak
and come netted and gasping in rainbow heaps,
or whether sun
will sit on yesterday's sparse scales
on the boat's floor.
               The day before
had poured an exuberance of fish
into tight nets. Arms had stretched
pulling them in, with hands deft,
dripping in sunlight
as they sorted and shifted baskets of ripples.
Even the market's brawl and clamor,
its stink of men with their beasts,
(with most of our catch given away)
was a happiness! What a time!
Especially that episode of the sinners!
Squinted against morning, James laughed,
recalling Levi's house,
whose robust company ate and drank and asked!
Asked? Enjoyed asking!
And took in fishermen and a jobless carpenter
easy as friends. Those Pharisees, now,
hard-eyed, tight — James wished

their law would eat them!
Well, Jesus had raised their backs
and they'd grumbled away.

                            Now the Sabbath sun,
day-fresh, had scoured the lake clean.
No wind wrinkled the water
to make it dark. And lean reeds
were still as sticks one by one
marking water's bound — or land's.
Vivid and quick from rest, impatient
for food, James flexed his strength,
broke lake's glass with a tossed stone,
and roared.

                          In an abundance
of jest and banter the company
munched meager bread
and made for the fertile plain of Gennesaret,
led by their strong-striding carpenter.
Wide fields of fair grain
glowing in noon, pomegranates like hung toys,
olive orchards grown aged
in silver and penumbral grace, opulent grapes,
those myriad breasts of the vine,
and blue-black figs, hidden, sweet —
this lush place was lined with life,
packed with it everywhere.
James, too, was filled. His face honeyed
from fruit, his belly at peace,
with a child's smile he fell asleep.

His pleasure smashed by a
grasp of voices, he came angry to afternoon heat,
his sweaty hands fisted,
his sleep-heavy sight blurred.
His carpenter spoke to a clump of crabbed Pharisees.
Pharisees? Asses! No, he rather favored asses.
Fish, then, with sharp snouts. Or vultures.
They did settle their mantles like wings,
and shook their hooked dark faces
at Jesus who was speaking,
quiet as a tree in his standing.
"The flowers appear on the earth,
and the time of singing.
Why fast, then? Isn't a bridegroom,
or a birth, to be feasted?
Wine new-made needs skins fresh as itself
to hold its sweetness.
Your laws will burst with the son of Man!
He spills over the land!
All days, even the Sabbath,
belong to him and God, not you!
To help, to sing praise, to enjoy!
Grief comes, but not yet!"
Jesus girded his tunic,
turned away, and set a fast pace
through locust-strident trees.
James came last, stumbling.
His mind held faces of cold hate and poison,
and he was afraid.

WHAT MANNER OF MAN?

A Roman centurion speaks:
Battle's indifference for this man or that
demands indifference. So I thought
until I saw him keep the field,
weaponless, before the arid legalists.
He yielded nothing of his ground
of devotion to growth under his God.
What a commander he could be in war!
His concern for enemies
far outreaches mine for slaves I love;
his siege needs more courage,
having no allegiances save from a few derelict
        fishermen;
and his mastership conquered Jupiter's fortress and me.

A man of Nain speaks:
Nobody comes to us much,
being so near Samaria
and not in touch with usual trade.
When we bore my sister's son, empty with death,
through gates of stone outside a sad city
and everyone came crying,
we met a straggled crowd of strangers
following a man.
His eyes and his hands
held our grief as if it were his
for that brief time.

What rose with his words
I'm not sure.
But the Lord God was in it, a marvel —
and he was such a young prophet.

A follower of the Baptist speaks:
John, scant, starved as a thorn-bush,
beat his bony fist on his knee,
his insistent eyes driving us from him
and Herod's prison down into Galilee.
We obeyed. Afraid much for him,
somewhat for us, we went under rules
of our fellowship. John's cousin
stood in a crowded village market, laughing,
when we found him.
Every sort of Jew clamored for hearing.
He listened to each, his sun-brown face
always in readiness to receive,
clear courtesy in his perceptive hands.
Lame, seeking, quarrelsome, blind or outcast —
whatever came he took as if grace
were given him and given back.
Many left with a look of freedom.
When we asked (for John)
was he that one expected, or should another be sought,
he spread his arms wide.
"See. And tell John what you see,
and you take no offense in me
for they do not."

He turned aside
to a solemn child's question.
We regained Jerusalem and John confused.
We never really knew.

A prostitute speaks:
I had forgotten childhood.
Its dew must have kissed me once,
but I had forgotten.
Beauty cursed me from birth,
and monstrous desire slew me,
poured my fire from a broken bowl.
Drop by drop my soul fell,
while owl's eyes watched
and wind sighed in cypresses.
I walked cold streets, shouted at brute shadows, holding
        a heart out.
I unraveled life, stitched
it again and liked it less.
Men were refuge from rain,
were malice, strife, and coin.
My loins were their rest,
my fame known, but no name.
I had forgotten childhood.
Then I saw him.
Torchlight shone around him.
It spilled a pool onto dirty stones in the street
and had a sound like bells.
Tell me, O tell me!

My naked feet took incoming upon themselves,
and the Pharisee (he knew me well)
let me pass, his countenance wrathful.
Did it matter?
Tides of years undone, tears ungiven carried me.
Words taught in childhood returned:
He brought me to the feast
and his banner over me was love.
I scarcely heard what this bright god
said to Pharisee and to me of sin and forgiveness.
I was witnessed as a truth
and I was a silent song!
I had forgotten childhood.
Since that night I am young.
I will follow him everywhere.

A friend speaks:
Sometimes the lines in his cheeks deepen,
his eyes are caverns, his hands shake,
and he paces the sable shore
in starlight until I fear for him.
Our lake breathes soft. Unsleeping, he sighs,
stops, stands pondering, then moves on,
a restless shadow by a resting sea.
What is his torment?
Do we not give strength enough, perhaps,
to help him hold our love?
When the length and spread of Galilee
is insistent that to lean is to live?

He is beside himself tonight,
as if he were astride a storm.

A Pharisee speaks:
Hating Rome, I have labored fifty years
to polish Moses' law for Israel.
The precise squares and triangles of synagogues
delineate God's home and raise Israel
above raw pagan stone.
My days declare justice,
and my eyes try defilement.
This shabby Nazarene is demon-infested,
bold beyond belief,
holding himself larger than Moses!
He is a thief of Jews,
yet dares to call us, the guardians,
to call us all blasphemers!
Surely he serves Satan.
We must observe him and publish him to Rome.

Another Nazarene speaks:
A strange boy, he never went roistering
as we did, parents shouting after us
over spring hills.
He wasn't prim, but as the eldest,
his father ill, he spent hours
in the carpenter shop
singing and working the wood.
He was lithe as a dark lamb.

On Sabbath he stopped in synagogue
to talk to rabbis, then walked home alone.
Toys he made us were gay,
but we understood nothing he said to us.
Three years he's been gone —
to some desert place, I'm told,
(after Joses was old enough).
His face is wiser, I suppose,
but his clothes are poor,
and he is still Joseph's son,
a Nazarene. Nothing more.

NO OR YES

Between Tiberias and Capernaum is a long uprise.
Our lake begins it, winds comb its top,
and spring grass is bright-splashed with anemone's
        blood,
white daisy dots, and spatters of yellow, blue and pink.
Shepherds bring lambing ewes to graze.
At sunset the lake fills with sails of homecoming
until a huge moon climbs over Decapolis.
                  Spent from recalling
intention and courage to men,
I climbed in a May twilight
onto this cool hill and slept.
The night swelled with Isaiah's high call:
Listen to me in silence,
O coastlands. Bring forth the people
who are blind, yet have eyes,
who are deaf, yet have ears.
Moon-spilled light drew together,
and I stood poised on a dream.
              I visioned my Jews
as a caravan of extremity marching a long road.
Each kind of man carried his blessing.
One beggar held a cup of roses.
Starveling children lifted loads of the land's food.
A woman twisted by tears bore a gay infant.
Stoned prophets wore king's robes,
while a rich ruler sat a horse of bones

and cradled a corpse.
Swollen with virtues and pride,
many entered a river-wide gate toward death.
A few turned toward life between strict stones
leading to unknown mountains.

Waking,
yearning to tell them of doves,
beasts, loneliness, love,
of a law of the indwelling God,
I said what I saw of choice and refusal,
of acts of holding and letting go,
of treasure found through No or Yes
spoken by man to God's facts.

Some heard, were bold and followed.

41

OUR LAKE IS A WOMAN

You sometimes say, Judas,
eyes veiled with strange humor,
that our lake is a woman
unfaithful and witch-wise
whose constancy weighs
only what it takes to tip a cloud.
You laugh loud and gesture a cup
with your great hands,
spilling her out.

A woman,
but not, Judas, to flout.
She is rose of Galilee on mild mornings;
and wild with passion
and purple shadows when cloud-scud
warns of early spring.
Cool as thin curved moon
which rings above her satin skin for May vespers,
she is virginal;
and awesome empress of dark
when summer stars circle her ways.
Even as death's mother
raging with hellish hunger,
she comes exalted;
visions are flung from her
and far echo the voices from her womb.
In last night's storm, Judas,

she offered me a choice
you wouldn't think of, being afraid.
The sky went out instantly,
our boats half-way across,
and we made sail in ink,
even the tiller-hands obscured.
The lake was disquiet,
filled with unsure pulses,
and stirred as one who dreams.
Weary from needs not mine, I slept
until you, my fishermen,
all unmanned by fright, crying of death, awoke me.
Wind screamed waves to fiends of foam,
black wine boiled over our bows,
we pitched and rose reeling
to slide the steep waters and up again,
prow first, proud! And you cried of death!
You could not see her,
lovely as a white lily
bending to storm's blast and boom,
robed in the blown spume,
still, and grave, and moving.
She held towards me a cup of silver light
set with stones bright as blood.
When my hands met hers the storm died,
and we rode under glitter of stars
on a silent sea.
If you do not trust her, Judas,
she will not let you be.

The sea shoved southeast, her waves blown
into blurred parabolas by a fierce wind.
Even to face the wind
footed and bent to the gusts
pushed a man's strength.
For unease and anger's sake I breasted
the wind wide open.
I spat dust to relieve me of something more;
the riddance pleased me.
Peter watched cornerly, his robe held close.
He wished, I guess,
that either I or the wind would stop but we did not,
and he stumbled impatiently,
half-breathed and in two minds.
"Why," he shouted into a hole in the wind,
"why not a sign? What's wrong with it?"

(O Peter, Peter! How constrained you are in the
bindings of natural things!
Your feet, now — dirty in their worn sandals —
do they ask evidence to walk?
Or your horny hands require a sign
before hauling the nets aboard?
Only the need, Peter,
only the need signifies itself!)
But I said nothing

— loathe to outroar the sea —
except, "There is no sign to give."

He was not glad.
Nor were those Pharisees who closed us in
near Capernaum. Wind had dropped;
air innocent again let us breathe free.
"Tell us how to know," they sought slyly.
"What sign?"

"Can you go how I go?
Through pain and the slow push out of darkness,
through burning, through clashes of choice
to the tomb as lonely as birth?
Earth you discern.
Learn there in fine-drawn frost,
in small tendrils of vine, and the sweep
of storks in spring, in grain full-eared.
The sign for us
is guilt undone in — somehow —
yes, in saving God
from our fettered and partial grace."

They left disgruntled.
Peter, his poor face twisted,
followed me wordless home.

ME, PETER

Since that hour on Hermon's flanks
my rabbi has altered. Even before,
he talked death and called me Satan —
me, Peter, whose concern is for his power,
not his thanks! What an awe he is!
But stubborn. He leads us to Jerusalem
with the flawed argument that no man,
having put his hand to the plough,
can turn back.
This is no stand to take, I say,
for him whose fortunes rise now
towards days of splendor.
Burning, his eyes deny me,
and he makes strange words about an exile,
son of Man, with no place to lay his head!

We go forward, village to village
along the Jordan full with spring.
Brief rain-slants drench us,
and sun pulls us dry and rings us
with peasant faces of pain and urgency.
My rabbi always listens.
His replies grow stringent, even to us.
Even speaking of prayer he chides us,
saying to ask, to seek,
to pound at God's door for bread!
Yet he is not in some wilderness

but with us who love him!
Sounds and smells are sweet
here in this valley — doves in fields,
green grain and trees blossoming,
wells rich with water. Why do his feet
not linger? He could be a king
by giving what our people desire!
Yet he talks of casting fire
as if he were in it,
as if his days were short and piercing
until some mystery happens.
I say "Rabbi, no!"
Fiercely he answers "Yes! Division, not peace, is mine."

So village to village we wind Jordan's valley
under a westerly breeze and clean skies,
fed by Perean earth,
free to please ourselves about coming and going,
yet tied to Jerusalem.
He heals on Sabbaths — most unwise —
and danger grows with fame.
He flashes replies as arrows from a bow
taut with intention. His name is reviled
by Pharisees everywhere and he bears it
— except that yesterday he cried out over Jerusalem,
hearing his life was sought.
His care was for this city's end, not his
nor ours — like a brooding hen
all of whose chicks were lost or dead.

He holds too much love, my rabbi.
He is tossed about on love
as on a rude sea.
If he keeps his head he may not drown in it.

We've followed half a moon in a sky of alabaster,
dawn alive with birds,
and turned across Jordan towards Jericho.
Cool hills give way to noon,
and we rest, we and all who came with us, under olive
        trees.
                    What does he say?
Why am I fear-filled?
In whose name must I hate wife, and parents
and my life? And why? What's free in this?
What fate led me here, to count what cost?
I will not cling to him to bear my cross!
He is my king till I die!

BLIND GUIDES

A brilliant city, Jerusalem,
glittering on its hills like a diamond
set in golden sand.
From the Jericho road it seems to fill the sky,
Herod's safeguard for Rome and for his god.
We crested the olive mountain.

With sunset in our eyes
we came to Kidron Valley
in the temple's shadows ragged and long.
A ewe called her straggling lamb.
From somewhere a camel driver's song
rested in still air and fell to earth.

How could I reach her heart,
this fabled city's heart,
to say the ways of birth before pride shattered her?
Would she again be scattered,
a prey to all established power's need?
The incessant cluster of Pharisees,
barrenly correct and wrapped
in righteousness and ancient law,
answered my questions by its own.
What I saw in their hate
was that bright loveless Jerusalem's fate
would be sealed by such men.

We entered the great gate as if to heal
were yet possible.

Nights we went out to Bethany
for peace from the city's desires.
Days we were about the business of the city,
a work of fire demanding my life's accomplishment
of freedom if God were to be free.
My friends took my way,
though reluctant to stand on my ground.

City of David, city of Solomon,
echoing sounds of a thousand years
and smelling of them all,
you are split by axes of might without love
and justice without man!
Empire to empire, taken and let go
and never quite routed,
you tell your pride in walls higher than God,
and match your wits to thralldom.
I flung courtyards of your temple
to a brassy sky yesterday —
doves, money, tables and men blowing
and flying like sand!
To ask after Isaiah
would have been expecting robbers to know equity!
And you into whose dry hands
my fate by now has passed,
you are pits for the unwary to stumble in!

You are masks over death, gates of iniquity
closed to the son of Man! You fit lies
to weakness! You adulterate the breath of God's days,
and will die with Jerusalem!

JUDAS

Impotent desert!
Only vipers sucking at bare hills!
Rocks ignite my eyes
and my blood burns into my bones!
Days, weeks, years — what has passed?

I turned once, I think,
and stumbled through all days — or none —
fast and slow, slow and fast . . .
. . . Men tried to stay me . . .
to give food . . . drink . . .
Here in this wild waste alone I could eat
. . . but sun drops fiery coins on my tongue
and sweat is salt!
Coins piled on coins, silver on silver,
higher than life . . . everywhere since Jerusalem
. . . on water . . .
in moonlight . . .
. . . held in olive trees . . .
but I left them there!
I gave them back, each one!
Each one!
I've run since before time
yet not outreached their blank indictment!
So, vulture, climb your hot sky and wait.
This stinking flesh will feed you soon enough!
O God . . . my bones bleach . . .

. . . I hate this flaming earth . . .
You made birth, not I . . .
. . . for a joke, I think . . .
I laugh at Your jackal, too,
his innocence eyeing my sin!
. . . I'll go his path . . .
but I must know why . . . Why?

How still within this heat . . .
. . . You, jackal, friend,
come soft over these rocks and bend your shade.
You fill me with remembering.
Your face is like his — wide-eyed, made in lines
     of truth —
("Whatever is given you in that hour,
speak that," he told us, his fine honesty
like yours standing beside us attentive.
"You will be hated," he said,
and I was bold and angry for that.
Our fate was to be kingship!)
. . . I mouth dust . . .
my hands wither, that gave the sign . . .
. . . a cool grave . . . I desire a place . . .
Your face — his face — holds mine in fire!
Gentle, jackal, come to me
where I rest, remembering.
That feast which was for joy
I made into a wound.
The advent he saw I avoided.

I risked him instead, laying plans for my freedom.
I meant to come
and kiss him then in that room but could not
. . . even as now my body is done with acts . . .
. . . nor could I taste the cup . . .
We were the only two . . .
. . . and he knew . . .
"One will betray," he said,
and passed unleavened bread to us all . . .

Father, God, Yahweh, Elohim!
Whoever You are . . . and if You are . . .
call down Your vulture!
This day . . . this terrible day . . .
. . . he is too close! . . .
His breath on my cheek . . .
. . . I kissed him as he left that garden!
Where did he go from Pilate?
. . . he wept once . . .
O weep for my empty death . . .
. . . and kiss me . . .

I DID NOT KNOW HIM

(1)

This garden was always an untroubled place of silenc
breathing cicadas and olive-silver wind recalling
    Galilee.
Not tonight.
Tonight space drowns me with noise of stars louder
    than my sea.
A faraway owl sounds frightened.
Passover bread is heavy in me
and the meager wine burns in my throat.
His head is dark against the star-shining sky.
I think he turns to see us.
Rabbi, master, my love is strong, believe me,
and if it's to be death I'll not deny, ever,
though you said I would!
For I caught my breath when you came, rain-drenched,
and shared our food by the lakeside.
You were tall; care touched your face
and warmed your eyes. You named me.
An unrecognized God you had,
and I followed in love.
All other existence I set by —
work on my surprising sea, home, wife, friends —
when my heart met your hallows
and fell to its knees.
Now night increases with an extension of stars and
    dread,

and though I tell myself that Jacob labored,
as you do, for a blessing
(and as I, Peter, must)
yet my head is reluctant . . .
 . . . Trust in a new day's breaking is thin
 . . . I hear my sin . . .
 . . . my sin was . . .
what was . . . my . . . sin . . .

(2)
Roused from bitter sleep into a chaos
of outcries, torches, striving men, I am dazed with
            disorder!
A servant lies bleeding!
A blaze of swords and staves are about us,
my ears ring,
my fear puts replies in my feet
beyond my choice!
His voice says
". . . power of darkness" . . . as I flee.

(3)
It is cold in this place.
No matter how heaped the fire it is cold.
My face aches, my hands feel old.
Sitting or standing, I tremble.
My desire exposes me,
and yet I had to come to be near my rabbi,
alone with his foes.

Creeping in shadows and love,
I moved behind their raucous righteous passage
under the city's blind eyes to this courtyard.
(O God, his God and mine!
They laugh! They make sport of him!
And Caiaphas will bulge with lies!)

"No, I only came for wine and warmth.
My feet were iced.
Galilee? Not I! Why should you recall Galilee?"

Twice she has asked.
She won't let me be still!
Nothing is still!
All Jerusalem cries crazily as if someone had died!
Dawn shivers with death
and a cock calls up the sun.

"No!
Save your breath! I did not know him!
(I love him!)
Let me go!"

A LONELY WINE

Since the night when I became new fledged
— like a bird I found once
and kept and fed till it could fly —
(he did the same for me)
since that night I've followed after,
not on the edge but in the midst of his company.
Sounds of my intention he heard for the first time,
and I was needed for what my hands could do
of seed-grinding, mending, gathering wood.
"Master," I'd say, "Don't mind
me washing your feet.
I'm no one, and not bold."
His smile, fuller than laughter,
told his regard for me.

        Now I stand anguished,
looking to that hill where death goes on
like a storm.
I took his worn sandals from soldiers who owed
        me kindness.
The sandals are strangers.
They pull me up the hard slope
nearer to a world's end.
He hoped we would hear his teaching
— to love and tend God, ourselves, and all men.
It should have been easy.
Why did chief priests, Romans,

even some of our own,
make him a thief and take him in the night?
You needed him, God!
What gave You such fright that You heeded Your
darkness?
He was saving Your life!
See, there like a flower red and brown
on a dead tree he hangs!
And where are You?
How many hours of pain will You have?
Sun falls on just and unjust.
I know. He told us.
And now he dies untimely.
He cries out You have forsaken!
What gain is this, God?
What yeast in Your poor loaf?
I feel You shudder!
May Your name be torn apart!

Acquit me, God, for that.
His darkening blood was shouting in my heart
and could not be borne.
Let us now bring him to the feast,
as he brought us.
Let us pour a lonely wine together.
Your need is even more than mine.

DIALOG OF THE CRUCIFIXION

Jesus:
God's dark glove was flung in my face
in those wild places beyond the Baptist,
where jackals raised moons, where vultures
brought sun and thirst, where I stared
into my people's mirrors and shouted "No!"
In those nights Adam's empty eye-sockets
filled with tears as I went with Cain
into wasteland; and Rebekah's hands
were on my shoulders and together we sang,
"Upon me be thy curse!"

God:
Doves are discoverers, I have observed,
of land and of love.
When my beloved leaps like a porpoise
from rippled waters to meet my spirit,
love is begotten.
For the first time. Always.
Heaven is a cloudy pearl and earth a sweet nut,
both glory-filled,
when such a birth opens me.

Jesus:
Dark valences of God bore hard upon my back since
        then,
drove me deeper into my genesis,

constrained me to seek the heart's treasure.
I asked of eyes in closed faces.
I asked of hands fisted and of ears sealed.
Restless, I kicked stones at a sea's edge
and let sea-smells and sea-work be my consorts.
Wide-staring glinting fish,
heads of grain singular as wrought gold,
grapes blood-colored, prodigal —
these were a wistful finitude on which I rested
from time to time between funerals of old gods
and the fiery making of this present sword.

God:
Omnipotence frightens me.
It swirls in amoeboid clouds until I feel lonely
and forsaken;
I reach out for help and I hear a cry
but cannot see what I do.
I need love again.
Always.
And forgiveness. Always.

Jesus:
God's sundered justice was a man paralyzed,
a woman of the streets,
was myself beside myself,
until desire and courage shattered roofs and law,
until importunate calls for compassion made
        compassion.

Man's bruised feet
and the opened eyes of God were washed and warmed
by tears which even now shine
in this day's black agony!

God:
Wisdom is newcome to my garden.
When I see her somehow I want to cry,
to stretch my arms everywhere
and gather creation into them. All of creation,
all the motley and iridescence of it,
its wonder and horror,
all mine.
Which is, perhaps, why I want to cry.
I long to hold it, to be in it and of it,
to partake of its multiform ugly beauty.
Wisdom teaches me my creation,
and her sad smile says how much I must learn.
Always.
Of loving and of being loved.
And fearing and being feared.
That, too. Always.

Jesus:
So many baptisms for man before God encompasses
         mercy!
I swam in rivers and repented;
I was burned by the terrible inward seeing
and its vision of night's unsleeping beasts;

I was frozen in cold power and hate;
immobility and fear ground me down.
Love slept in cruel silence,
while I beat my hands on God's door
and it opened and God and I
saw our needs and exchanged our gifts
in the olive garden!

God:
Unless I am awakened my bread grows stale,
my heaviness pulls me,
my beloved is forgotten.
Yet that son who rouses me wounds me,
and is wounded by my weight, and dies.
Always.
And I, always,
must absorb his agony into myself as mine,
to raise me to larger memory
and mercy and farther seeing.
I must hold his darkness in my heart,
sleepless and weeping,
until I am illumined and revealed to myself
as richer than I could have known.